© **JOVIAL JUNE**
BY SANDEEP RAVIDUTT SHARMA

Table of Contents

Foreword IV

JOVIAL JUNE..1

© JOVIAL JUNE
BY SANDEEP RAVIDUTT SHARMA

Foreword

This book provides you with a list of 100 quotes and thoughts about LIFE, churned out by my mind with the consciousness, grace and energy of Shiva Shakti. I'm sure if you keep reading, referring, sharing these thoughts and quotes about LIFE, you may derive inspiration and develop good understanding of various perspectives and facts. When you look for good things in life, it helps to automatically pull all the positivity in and around you. Life appears amazing and becomes beautiful.

"With your jovial outlook, you can make this world a better place not just to live but to thrive with a smile."

I sincerely hope, you will find this book amazing, interesting, rejuvenating, unique and a constant source of inspiration.

Thank You and Happy Reading.

© JOVIAL JUNE
BY SANDEEP RAVIDUTT SHARMA

© Copyright 2018 Sandeep Ravidutt Sharma - All rights reserved.
In no way is it legal to reproduce, duplicate, or transmit any part of this document in either electronic means or in printed format. Recording of this publication is strictly prohibited and any storage of this document is not allowed unless with written permission from the publisher. All rights reserved. The information provided herein is stated to be truthful and consistent, in that any liability, in terms of inattention or otherwise, by any usage or abuse of any policies, processes, or directions contained within is the solitary and utter responsibility of the recipient reader. Under no circumstances will any legal responsibility or blame be held against the author / publisher for any reparation, damages, or monetary loss due to the information herein, either directly or indirectly. The author own all copyrights.

Legal Notice:
This book is copyright protected. This is only for personal use. You cannot amend, distribute, sell, use, quote or paraphrase any part or the content within this book without the consent of the author or copyright owner. Legal action will be pursued if this is breached.

Disclaimer Notice:
Please note the information contained within this book is for motivational, educational and knowledge sharing purpose only. Every attempt has been made to provide the reader accurate, up to date and reliable complete information. No warranties of any kind are expressed or implied. Readers acknowledge that the author is not engaging in the rendering of legal, financial, medical or professional advice. By reading this document, the reader agrees that under no circumstances the author / publisher is responsible for any losses, direct or indirect, which are incurred as a result of the use of information contained within this document, including, but not limited to, —errors, omissions, or inaccuracies.

If you have further questions, contact on **Tel: +919969256731**
Email: sandeepraviduttsharma@gmail.com

© **JOVIAL JUNE**
BY SANDEEP RAVIDUTT SHARMA

Dedication

This book is dedicated to **Shiva Shakti** - the epitome of love. Lord Shiva is pure consciousness symbolising the masculine principle. Goddess Shakti symbolises the active feminine energy of Shiva and is synonymously identified with **Tripura Sundari, Sati** or **Parvati**.

These primal principles are also called as PURUSHA representing consciousness and PRAKRITI denoting the nature. Shiva and Shakti are manifestations of the all-in-one divine consciousness. Shiva is the paternal love of God that gives us consciousness, knowledge and clarity. Shakti is the motherly love of God that showers warmth, care and ensures our protection. Shiva and Shakti exist within each of us as the masculine and feminine energy. To please **Shiva Shakti** praying for the well being, love, happiness, strength, positive energy and success of my readers in their life, I hereby recite the following mantra...

"Sarva Mangala Mangalye Shive Sarvartha Sadhike Sharanye Tryambake Gauri Narayani Namostute"

JOVIAL JUNE

© **JOVIAL JUNE**
BY SANDEEP RAVIDUTT SHARMA

Don't let fear hold you back when Courage is calling you.

© **JOVIAL JUNE**
BY SANDEEP RAVIDUTT SHARMA

Wonderful are the ways of the Lord. You decide to walk and he makes you run.

© JOVIAL JUNE
BY SANDEEP RAVIDUTT SHARMA

Simplicity finds answers to all kinds of complexities.

© JOVIAL JUNE
BY SANDEEP RAVIDUTT SHARMA

Think good and life will be amazing.

© JOVIAL JUNE
BY SANDEEP RAVIDUTT SHARMA

We hardly know anything about this world forget about knowing the creator.

© JOVIAL JUNE
BY SANDEEP RAVIDUTT SHARMA

Innovators can tell you how each failure has contributed to their innovation. After every failure you never forget to try again.

© **JOVIAL JUNE**
BY SANDEEP RAVIDUTT SHARMA

Raise your voice loud enough for everyone to hear what you have to say. For this don't just climb the terrace.

© **JOVIAL JUNE**
BY SANDEEP RAVIDUTT SHARMA

Be the motivation for living a joyful life.

© **JOVIAL JUNE**
BY SANDEEP RAVIDUTT SHARMA

Try not to panic when you find yourself completely helpless. Leave it to TIME and keep patience.

© **JOVIAL JUNE**
BY SANDEEP RAVIDUTT SHARMA

The one who is ready to give good can very well qualify to get the best.

© **JOVIAL JUNE**
BY SANDEEP RAVIDUTT SHARMA

Don't try to influence the results through different means except your scintillating performance.

© **JOVIAL JUNE**
BY SANDEEP RAVIDUTT SHARMA

Temporary solutions create permanent problems. Look at the root and cure the cause.

© **JOVIAL JUNE**
BY SANDEEP RAVIDUTT SHARMA

Pain and suffering test your resolve.

© **JOVIAL JUNE**
BY SANDEEP RAVIDUTT SHARMA

You can surpass your limitations by staying focused.

© **JOVIAL JUNE**
BY SANDEEP RAVIDUTT SHARMA

Nothing changes in this world unless you do.

© **JOVIAL JUNE**
BY SANDEEP RAVIDUTT SHARMA

Positivity needs frequent reinforcement.

© JOVIAL JUNE
BY SANDEEP RAVIDUTT SHARMA

Don't auction your happiness to earn few grains of Gold.

© **JOVIAL JUNE**
BY SANDEEP RAVIDUTT SHARMA

Those who practice gratitude is sure to know the worth of others contribution.

Everyone likes to look smart, very few actually find ways to become one.

© JOVIAL JUNE
BY SANDEEP RAVIDUTT SHARMA

Shed the baggage of your past if you want to give your best today.

© **JOVIAL JUNE**
BY SANDEEP RAVIDUTT SHARMA

Eliminate distraction by just focusing on your task and you can win.

© **JOVIAL JUNE**
BY SANDEEP RAVIDUTT SHARMA

Great places await those who dare to explore.

© JOVIAL JUNE
BY SANDEEP RAVIDUTT SHARMA

Don't try to push the most critical task at the end else just the thought of it would eat up your time. Face the most challenging task first and the smaller ones would never raise their head.

Those who work hard should look for smart ways to do.

© JOVIAL JUNE
BY SANDEEP RAVIDUTT SHARMA

To look good you can't change the mirror. Change starts from within.

© JOVIAL JUNE
BY SANDEEP RAVIDUTT SHARMA

Thank you dear Lord for answering our prayers and showering your choicest blessings.

© **JOVIAL JUNE**
BY SANDEEP RAVIDUTT SHARMA

Avoid unrealistic goal setting to make the most of your resources.

© **JOVIAL JUNE**
BY SANDEEP RAVIDUTT SHARMA

Be ready to face challenges in life.

© JOVIAL JUNE
BY SANDEEP RAVIDUTT SHARMA

Those who are interested in learning more will find newer ways to explore.

© **JOVIAL JUNE**
BY SANDEEP RAVIDUTT SHARMA

Attract happiness through kindness and compassion.

© **JOVIAL JUNE**
BY SANDEEP RAVIDUTT SHARMA

Everything will change the day you change your attitude and embrace positive thinking.

© **JOVIAL JUNE**
BY SANDEEP RAVIDUTT SHARMA

Find courage to rise again from the Ocean of sorrow.

© **JOVIAL JUNE**
BY SANDEEP RAVIDUTT SHARMA

A hundred lies are not good enough to conceal single truth for long.

© **JOVIAL JUNE**
BY SANDEEP RAVIDUTT SHARMA

Life comes to a full circle when you are beaten at your own game.

© **JOVIAL JUNE**
BY SANDEEP RAVIDUTT SHARMA

Don't bother about how others plan to win the game. It's better that you focus on your own plan and strategy.

© **JOVIAL JUNE**
BY SANDEEP RAVIDUTT SHARMA

Those who value time always reach early and are present when the opportunity knocks.

Each improved step moves you closer to greater success.

© JOVIAL JUNE
BY SANDEEP RAVIDUTT SHARMA

Value freedom.

© **JOVIAL JUNE**
BY SANDEEP RAVIDUTT SHARMA

Dreams drive you, or you are happy driving dreams.

© JOVIAL JUNE
BY SANDEEP RAVIDUTT SHARMA

Persistent efforts always pay.

© **JOVIAL JUNE**
BY SANDEEP RAVIDUTT SHARMA

With your eyes you can pick up Gold or dust. Knowledge matters.

© **JOVIAL JUNE**
BY SANDEEP RAVIDUTT SHARMA

Hold the hand of love with complete trust and surrender.

© JOVIAL JUNE
BY SANDEEP RAVIDUTT SHARMA

Touch the shore and feel the Sea. You never know when the next voyage calls for you.

© JOVIAL JUNE
BY SANDEEP RAVIDUTT SHARMA

Translate your likeness into the words of appreciation, and you have motivated the other.

© JOVIAL JUNE
BY SANDEEP RAVIDUTT SHARMA

Fly high if you aim to touch the Sky.

© **JOVIAL JUNE**
BY SANDEEP RAVIDUTT SHARMA

Don't fall flat when people criticise you, get up to sort out the shortcomings and rise again proving them wrong.

© JOVIAL JUNE
BY SANDEEP RAVIDUTT SHARMA

Don't fail to succeed when you are so close to it. Get going with the extra dose of efforts and success is all yours.

© JOVIAL JUNE
BY SANDEEP RAVIDUTT SHARMA

Walk an extra mile today if you plan to relax tomorrow.

© JOVIAL JUNE
BY SANDEEP RAVIDUTT SHARMA

Set realistic goals which can #motivate you.

© JOVIAL JUNE
BY SANDEEP RAVIDUTT SHARMA

Using big words can enhance your image but simple words can make others understand.

© **JOVIAL JUNE**
BY SANDEEP RAVIDUTT SHARMA

Make people realise where they are going wrong to put them back on the right track and not with the intention to score over them.

© JOVIAL JUNE
BY SANDEEP RAVIDUTT SHARMA

Declare your intentions and let others decide whether they are noble or not.

© **JOVIAL JUNE**
BY SANDEEP RAVIDUTT SHARMA

Don't just buy Silence when you intend to entertain.

© **JOVIAL JUNE**
BY SANDEEP RAVIDUTT SHARMA

Life challenges you every minute. The one which doesn't challenge you is not life.

© JOVIAL JUNE
BY SANDEEP RAVIDUTT SHARMA

Master patience and wait no longer would seem to be a burden.

To deal with complexity of an issue, all you have to do is think simple and divide it into smaller goals to achieve arranged in proper sequence to execute.

© JOVIAL JUNE
BY SANDEEP RAVIDUTT SHARMA

Going forward you may need favour from lessons learnt in the past.

© JOVIAL JUNE
BY SANDEEP RAVIDUTT SHARMA

You are the greatest gift of the Lord to the mankind. Live up to your reputation.

© JOVIAL JUNE
BY SANDEEP RAVIDUTT SHARMA

Don't get upset because things turned against you. Dream again and this time set things with positive attitude and workable plan.

Not everyone can understand the depth of your words. Keep trying to convey differently.

© JOVIAL JUNE
BY SANDEEP RAVIDUTT SHARMA

Relationship blooms in the Sunshine of trust and rainbow of love.

© **JOVIAL JUNE**
BY SANDEEP RAVIDUTT SHARMA

There is no way one can hide happiness. It has to appear as your Smile.

© JOVIAL JUNE
BY SANDEEP RAVIDUTT SHARMA

Nothing rules your mind when you meditate.

Fold your yesterday to see your today which is busing unfolding your tomorrow.

© **JOVIAL JUNE**
BY SANDEEP RAVIDUTT SHARMA

Value contribution of others in your win however small it may be.

© **JOVIAL JUNE**
BY SANDEEP RAVIDUTT SHARMA

Don't turn back when it's time to fight.

© JOVIAL JUNE
BY SANDEEP RAVIDUTT SHARMA

Invest your dreams by trusting your efforts to reap the dividend of SUCCESS.

© JOVIAL JUNE
BY SANDEEP RAVIDUTT SHARMA

Refine your thought with a touch of positivity. You will see amazement.

© **JOVIAL JUNE**
BY SANDEEP RAVIDUTT SHARMA

Accept the riches and pain alike. That's what life has to offer.

© **JOVIAL JUNE**
BY SANDEEP RAVIDUTT SHARMA

Add deeds to your voice and you gain trust of all.

© JOVIAL JUNE
BY SANDEEP RAVIDUTT SHARMA

It hardly matters if what you said is spoken differently by the other but conveys the same thing.

© **JOVIAL JUNE**
BY SANDEEP RAVIDUTT SHARMA

Rescue your self from the roaring storm of thoughts by staying calm and ignoring them. Think but do not over think.

© JOVIAL JUNE
BY SANDEEP RAVIDUTT SHARMA

Never mind if someone acts stupid just to bring the smile on your face.

© **JOVIAL JUNE**
BY SANDEEP RAVIDUTT SHARMA

You can't change the beginning but with your positive attitude can very well influence the world.

© **JOVIAL JUNE**
BY SANDEEP RAVIDUTT SHARMA

Light the lamp not to drive away the darkness but to illuminate your world.

© JOVIAL JUNE
BY SANDEEP RAVIDUTT SHARMA

Win people and not just the jobs they offer you.

© **JOVIAL JUNE**
BY SANDEEP RAVIDUTT SHARMA

The amazing world is within your reach.

© **JOVIAL JUNE**
BY SANDEEP RAVIDUTT SHARMA

Unclutter your mind by inviting focus to stay with you.

Rebuild your life this time on the foundation of good thoughts.

© JOVIAL JUNE
BY SANDEEP RAVIDUTT SHARMA

Don't speak if silence has conveyed your thoughts and opinion.

© JOVIAL JUNE
BY SANDEEP RAVIDUTT SHARMA

Positive thinking helps one to discover way where there existed none.

© JOVIAL JUNE
BY SANDEEP RAVIDUTT SHARMA

Chase your dreams in the right lane.

© JOVIAL JUNE
BY SANDEEP RAVIDUTT SHARMA

Hold on to your determination with rope of confidence, you will make it to the winners gallery.

© **JOVIAL JUNE**
BY SANDEEP RAVIDUTT SHARMA

Create a happy world with your good thoughts and kind deeds.

© JOVIAL JUNE
BY SANDEEP RAVIDUTT SHARMA

Celebrate your journey, and you will find your destination marked with excitement and jubilation.

© JOVIAL JUNE
BY SANDEEP RAVIDUTT SHARMA

Don't let your past steal your future. Stay in the present.

© **JOVIAL JUNE**
BY SANDEEP RAVIDUTT SHARMA

When Curiosity doesn't let you sleep, it means you are learning and are eager to know what next.

© **JOVIAL JUNE**
BY SANDEEP RAVIDUTT SHARMA

Be the change and amaze the World.

© JOVIAL JUNE
BY SANDEEP RAVIDUTT SHARMA

Everything will be fine. Have self-belief.

Transform your thoughts into words or deeds is all up to you.

© JOVIAL JUNE
BY SANDEEP RAVIDUTT SHARMA

Silence holds many words beneath.

© **JOVIAL JUNE**
BY SANDEEP RAVIDUTT SHARMA

Sometimes you can't make out what is right or wrong. Leave it to time and you will soon know.

© JOVIAL JUNE
BY SANDEEP RAVIDUTT SHARMA

Kindhearted person doesn't need an introduction.

© JOVIAL JUNE
BY SANDEEP RAVIDUTT SHARMA

Your choice of words has the power to please or make one sick. Choose wisely.

© JOVIAL JUNE
BY SANDEEP RAVIDUTT SHARMA

Victory plays hide n seek when you are not sure about your next step forward.

© **JOVIAL JUNE**
BY SANDEEP RAVIDUTT SHARMA

Just listen to music with complete focus, and it unclutters your mind.

© **JOVIAL JUNE**
BY SANDEEP RAVIDUTT SHARMA

Delegate responsibilities if you are leading a team but remember to monitor the outcome.

© JOVIAL JUNE
BY SANDEEP RAVIDUTT SHARMA

Appreciate the gift of good thoughts and do remember to share with others.

Everything will be alright.
Trust the Lord.

> © **JOVIAL JUNE**
> BY SANDEEP RAVIDUTT SHARMA

Don't live in your dreams when reality keeps calling.

Words influences your mindset, actions and can make you a winner.

Read books authored by Sandeep Ravidutt Sharma and get your daily dose of motivation.

sandeepraviduttsharma@gmail.com

www.ingramcontent.com/pod-product-compliance
Lightning Source LLC
Chambersburg PA
CBHW031440210526
45464CB00005B/2272